THE PREACHER
AND THE
First Lady

MARGARET FOUNTAIN COLEMAN

ISBN 979-8-88616-093-2 (paperback)
ISBN 979-8-88616-094-9 (digital)

Christian Faith Publishing
832 Park Avenue
Meadville, PA 16335
www.christianfaithpublishing.com

Printed in the United States of America

CONTENTS

THE FIRST LADY PHENOMENA IS ME

THE BOOK OF Proverbs concludes with a proverbial poem to King Lemuel, which his mother taught him. This particular proverb contains a powerful message. Lady Wisdom reappears in the crescendo of the book, describing a virtuous woman. Some translators use "wife" instead of "woman," probably because the woman's husband and children are mentioned in the passage. (Both "wife" and "woman" are possible translations of the Hebrew *ishshah*.)[1]

> Who can find a virtuous and capable woman?
> She is more precious than rubies. Her husband
> can trust her, and she will greatly enrich his life.
> She brings him good not harm all the days of her
> life. (Proverbs 31:10–12)

Proverbs 31 is a remarkable text. It is one of the most celebrated texts, highlighting a woman's strength, her unselfishness, and her accountability to her family. Many preachers, both male and female, use this particular pericope of the thirty-first chapter for Mother's Day and Women's Day services. No doubt, I would rank this as being

---

[1] NAS Exhaustive Concordance of the Bible with Hebrew-Aramaic and Greek Dictionaries, copyright © 1981, 1998 by The Lockman Foundation, all rights reserved Lockman.org.

the most used and overused text in the Bible for these occasions. The imagery of this woman can be interpreted in many ways.

Male preachers quite often view this text as the gold standard of what a woman and/or wife should be modeled as. This woman depicted in the text can do it all. Within a patriarchal mindset, this model wife and mother's value is viewed high because she puts her family above anything else, including herself. She will make sure everyone else is good before attending to her needs. To begin this section of the pericope, describing her first relationship with her husband, symbolizes her relationship priority. Although the scribed does not outrightly say that the woman sees her husband as her first priority, it is most definitely a relationship of great importance to the woman who is being illuminated. And since projection is a thing, many proclaimers pinpoint this part of the text to elevate what an exemplary woman she represents. She exemplified the pristineness of womanhood and motherhood.

Similarly, women preachers find the strength of the Proverbs woman just as notable and remarkable. Most women preachers often take a more liberating approach in analyzing and exegeting the text. Many of my colleagues, including myself, have engaged this particular text from the lens of both feministic and womanist theological thought. Many see this woman as an entrepreneur, a warrior, self-reliant, resilient, capable. She is the biblical manifestation of the 1978 Enjoli perfume commercial jingle that contained the iconic line: "I can bring home the bacon, fry it up in a pan."

The Enjoli perfume commercial was marketed to portray the feminist superwoman. In particular, the commercial featured a modern career woman who represented various roles over the course of a day. The critique of the commercial presented a phenomenal woman. This multifaceted woman could bring home the bacon, meaning she could earn a living. She could fry it up in a pan, which meant that she could attend to her domestic responsibilities as well. This strong woman's persona ends with her dressed in an evening gown as she sings that she never lets anyone forget who she is. This take-charge woman would be representative of the Proverbs 31 woman.

Liken to the commercial, as well as the biblical text, contained in Proverbs 31, it is not unusual for women to morph in attempting to model or mold themselves into these critiques. Seemingly, I can see how biblical text and its aspects are modeled in many contextual nuances of life. As this work was birthed, I prepared by talking with a few First Ladies in congregations since this position was a new experience for me. I remember vividly long conversations with many women, and they were providing me the skinny of this new-lived reality that I was now embarking into. So the preface of the conversations was now beginning to take form, and I knew, like anything else, that I would take what would benefit me and then leave the rest on the table.

Many of the First Ladies that I've encountered over the years have been women with quiet dispositions. These ladies would ordinarily serve in the background of their husband's ministries. I can remember the First Lady from my childhood church. She would sit on the same pew each Sunday, poised with hat and gloves. She would sit near the deaconess. She was unassuming and blended into the congregation. There wasn't any over-the-top attention given to her. So if you were a casual visitor, you wouldn't even know who she was. I really didn't see that as an issue; but as I became more involved in the life of the church, it was becoming even more odd that the First Lady was just the wife of the pastor, and her sole responsibilities was to be his wife and raise their children. It was an interesting dynamic to say the least.

When I left for undergraduate school in the early 1980s in the urban area of Richmond, Virginia, I didn't allow my church life to end. Attending an urban Baptist Church definitely was quite different than the rural experiences of my childhood. Although I wasn't astute enough to critique the dynamics of ministries, I was early on interested in or focused on with interest the relationship of the First Lady and the congregation. Why, at the time that would spark my curiosity, would now become clearer now that I serve in that position presently? I watched with amazement.

The First Ladies I've encountered were doers. They worked alongside their husbands. They collaborated with the women's ministries of their respective churches. Although their demeanor for most often remained reserved, they seemed to have more of a self-awareness that their voice in ministry was needed and respected. First Ladies, during this time of my church awakening, represented for many their relevance in the household of faith. I viewed this as empowering, knowing that a woman could have such an impressive presence in the church.

So as I've grown in church life, the ethos of what a First Lady should represent has evolved. Not to weigh this particular reading down in the weightiness of First Lady etiquette, this book serves a unique purpose. For those who don't know, I'm not only a First Lady, but I'm also an ordained minister and founder of my own ministry. I married a pastor who has been serving congregations for more than forty years. He is entrenched in his role as pastor. I, however, taking on the role as First Lady at the onset, was definitely daunting, and at times, my prophetic mantle did not jive well with my First Lady role. Geesh!

As life would have it, I met the office as First Lady with humility. However, as the years went on, I began to dislike and, at some times, loathe the office and the title. It became apparent to me that I was often treated by some as an ornament for my husband. People were more interested in my outfit and my big hat rather than the ministry gifts that operated within me. Needless to say, the office and ministry of First Lady were something I definitely had to grow and mature into. But enough about my journey. This book serves to bring revelation and reality of struggles that are faced by First Ladies. The collection of stories is introduced by sermons I've preached over the years.

Within any biblical story, we can find common experiences that parallel with our life experiences—so true for the unique experiences of women within the Holy Writ. From Eve's story of misguidance to Mary's story of being called to an extraordinary task, we all can find a window to peer into that compels us to take a deeper dive into how this mirrors our own life experiences. The sermon's reflected sets a framework in showing how a name substitution could in reality be your story. So as you meet the Samaritan woman and First Lady

Barbara; Hannah and First Lady Michelle; Queen Vashti and First Lady Tonia; a father, a daughter, a woman with a blood issue and First Lady Shana; take time to reflect to become one with the experiences and draw out how to find your wholeness in their stories.

CHAPTER 1

THE PREACHER PROCLAIMS: THIS IS MY STORY!

*Then leaving her water jar, the woman went back
to the town and said to the people, Come, see
a man who told me everything I ever did.*

—John 4:28-29 NIV

COULD THIS BE the Messiah?

Reality TV is not as real as you may think. No matter how real the characters portray their lives, the show still must produce a set of ratings to draw in viewer interest as well as sponsorship and endorsements. The real-life actors are under a sizable contract and realize that the more they sell sensationalism and market over the top behaviors, the more we, as the viewers/consumers, will tune in, and the show ratings will skyrocket. We get hooked on shows that exhibit marriage drama; we get spellbound with people exposing the intimate details of their lives as well as the desperate attempts to normalize a seemingly dysfunctional reality. We get hooked. But why?

It is my belief that, for many, we get hooked or engaged in these melodramas for various reasons: Some may have become interested because of boredom, some because of escapism, or sometimes simply because one may not want to think about their own complicated lives. It is easier to escape in the drama of someone else's chaos, confusion, problems, or situations than to deal with what is happening in one's own life. However, this type of escapism unfortunately does not bring about the longevity of relief that one may be looking for. So it becomes an internal drumbeat to stop hiding in the shadows of other people's stories and become real with yourself.

In the body of Christ, many of us should be at a place of maturity in our lives that we don't want to immerse ourselves in television antics, lifetime tragedies, or reality television drama as an escape or to use to water down the complexities of own lives. It is time to look at our own lives, our own narrative, to see that we are "real-life living." There are no rose-colored glasses to look through; the smoke-and-mirrors concept now has to be revealed; and deflection is not an option.

At some point, we have to rid ourselves from the makeup, hiding the puffiness of our eyes because we've cried all night long. We must shed the clothing concealing the abuse perpetrated on our bodies. We must free ourselves of the exhaustion of wearing that fake smile that hides the pain of everyday living. Many of us have been in that place where we must face reality; come to grips to what is clearly right in front of our faces.

The reality is, life isn't that great! Money is funny; children are crazy; your significant other has flipped the script of the relationship; your job is at a dead end; and the more you seem to do to make things manageable, the more it seems that you are getting deeper and deeper into the depths of a reality TV episode. Quick fixes can't solve the problem anymore. Avoidance can't escape the situation. And to add insult to injury, you just can't catch a break. So in case this is you, I want this prophetic word from God to serve notice that "your reality has been put on blast, and now you have to come face-to-face with your story!"

We all have a story to tell, a story to witness too, a story to reveal. However, if truth be told, it is scary to have your story exposed. It is frightening to have people become privy to the uncut version of your life. See when you've kept up appearances for appearances' sake and you've remained true to the facade, it is hard to allow what you have built up as your persona to become open for public viewing as it comes tumbling down.

In our text, a woman's reality of life begins to unfold. Now being who we are, everyone thought they knew her story. Everybody in the neighborhood talked about her life as if they had firsthand knowledge. You know how it is. The text references her by ethnicity rather than her name. She is not known by her name; she was identified by cultural framing. We don't know if her name was Mary, Karin, or LaTisha. No, she was purposefully indicated at this point by cultural ethnicity and gender. It is my belief that the scribe believed that this was all that we needed to know in order to get the gist of the encounter.

I know some of us can relate when, who we are—our God given birth name—has no relevance. We painfully become called by our situation, defined by our problem. We've all been there. You are no longer who Mommy and Daddy named you. Your government name is inconsequential. The given name has now been replaced with what you've been called on the streets. Your given name has been substituted with the lifestyle you may be presently engaged in. Your given name is now omitted, characterized by what you use to do or be. I know what I am referencing. Instead of Larry, they call you convict. Instead of Jackie, they call you addict. Instead of Steve, they call you the town liar. Instead of Sara, they call you victim. Instead of Mike or Latisha, they call you the one who sleeps around. The world calls you failure, unworthy, or disgraced. The world calls you by your predicament and not by your promise. The world calls you by your circumstance and not by your purpose.

So our biblical scene has us being introduced to a woman, a Samaritan, who was on her way to the community well at the heat of the day. This is particularly interesting because she waited until the heat of the day to arrive at the well when, by most household norms, water was probably drawn in the mornings for a variety of reasons. Just the mere essential usage of water would suggest that it would be necessary to have your waterpots filled and accessible to complete the daily chores and routines of the household for that given day.

But I want to suggest to you that the timing of her journey is important. The heat of the day, which most scholars suggest would be noonday, was the elected time that she went to the well. Her attention was just to get a pot of water. Although the text does not say why she came at that time, we can infer that she came out of sense of need, yes, but also avoidance. This would be the time, most likely, other women would be taking care of their daily chores and routines at their respective homes. This would be the time that the men were about their business doing their trade. This would be the time that the children may have been playing or doing just what children do. Yet she chose this time so that she would be undetected from the whispers, glares, and snickers of her so-called neighbors and even her friends.

Can you imagine what she may had been enduring?—the talk of the town; people sizing her up, believing they knew more about her life story than she did. I can just imagine that daughters were being warned to stay their distance so that they wouldn't be associated with her. Sons were being told she was not worthy to be looked upon. This woman waited to quench her need until she believed that the gossipers and the onlookers were all tucked away in their homes. She waited until the heat of the day, the sixth hour to go.

Her motive to get there, even at the heat of the day, was out of necessity. Necessity every now and again will motivate you. Perhaps she was thirsty and was motivated to quench her thirst. Perhaps she was motivated to get the last of her chores done. Perhaps she was motivated because she was down to the last ounce of water in the house. Whatever was happening with her, she continued her course, motivated to get to the well for water.

The trip to the well was a story. Just the motivation to get there and the necessity of having to go could fill the pages of this sermon. But girlfriend had to go. She had to make the trip. Unbeknown to her though, she was about to write a new chapter in her personal novel. As she got closer to the well, looking ahead to ensure that no one was there, she spotted from the distance a figure sitting by the well, an unexpected figure. And as she got closer, she saw that it was a man she did not recognize. I would suspect that she probably thought about retreating or turning back. But the second thought came. This man, as she recognized from afar, was not a Samaritan; he was a Jew. And how did she know that from far off? His clothing had to be the indication or the hue of his skin. Something identifiable caused the woman to know that this man did not belong.

By the mere fact of identifying him as a Jew, this man could not engage her anyway, so the likelihood of an exchange was highly unlikely. So without apprehension, she continued the walk so that she could complete her task at the well.

Now with these set of facts alone, this scene should have ended this passage. However, the story line was just unfolding. As this woman gets to the well, this man whom she assumed would retreat, beat a hasty exit, spoke to her. He asked her to give him a drink. And note, there were no formal introductions. The stranger never introduced himself. He allowed the woman to reference him as sir.

And at this point, the contact was made. He asked our lady for a drink. She was puzzled by the question. This woman could not believe her ears! Had he forgotten that he was in Samaria? Maybe he did not recognize her as a Samaritan. The Samaritans lived in the land that once belonged to Ephraim and Manasseh in Israel. Their capital was Samaria, a city occupied by people from a wide variety of nations after the defeat of Israel by Assyria mentioned in 2 Kings 17:24.

Over time, the remaining Israelites married foreigners who served other gods. Samaritan religion grew to become a mixture of pagan worship with variations of worship of the Lord (2 Kings 17:26–28). The Jewish people looked down on Samaritans and had little to do with them for several reasons: their mixed ethnicity, their ignorance and disregard of the ways of God, and their worship of God on Mount Gerizim instead of at the temple in Jerusalem.

Jacob's well, the communal place where necessity, was met. Both Jesus and the Samaritan woman came out of necessity, yet her necessity would be more than a physiological need. This encounter would bear witness that God is not a respecter of person. When God sees a need, He will meet you at your well experience. When God sees a need, He will meet you at any time and at any place. When God sees a need, He does not conform to religious, ethnic, or cultural correctness. He intervenes. He detours. He intersects. When

He recognizes that healing is needed, when He finds that deliverance and transformation is needed, He is right there.

Jesus responded, "If you knew the gift of God and who it is who says to you, 'Give me a drink,' you would have asked Him, and He would have given you living water" (John 4:10 NLT).

The woman responded based on her cultural and physiological understanding of their interaction. "But, sir, you don't have a rope or a bucket," she said. "And this well is very deep. Where would you get this living water? And besides, do you think you're greater than our ancestors Jacob, who gave us this well? How can you offer better water than he and his sons and his animals enjoyed" (John 4:11–12 NLT)?

Jesus continued the conversation with her by explaining what the real necessity of her trip was about on this day. It wasn't just a walkout of a physical need. This was not coincidental encounter but an intentional encounter on a hot day. Jesus replied, "Anyone who drinks this water will soon become thirsty again. But those who drink the water I give will never be thirsty again. It becomes a fresh, bubbling spring within them, giving them eternal life" (John 4:13–14 NLT).

Jesus was providing for her the real necessity of her trip and the real story behind her thirstiness. See, when we focus on the physiological aspects of our lives, we will often find ourselves remaining thirsty. Jesus needed our sister to understand that the water from the well was a temporary thirst quencher, but what he had to offer was an ever-flowing and overflowing thirst reliever. You will never thirst again!

Do you understand what this is like? Finally, after searching for something to fill the void, something to complete you, Jesus had it in the well of God's spiritual water. It not only fills you, but it will cause you to walk in the overflow. It will complete you and then spill over on your circumstances. It will spill over on your family and your friends. It is overflowing, and it is the ever-flowing power of God's Spirit.

Although Jesus had her fully captivated, he knew that there were details of her life that blocked complete fullness and wholeness. Jesus requested that the woman go home and bring her husband back with her. The woman spoke out of the reality of her situation: she had no husband. Jesus, in His request, needed her to see the reality of her motive for her trip to the well daily at the heat of the day and the necessity of not just quenching her physical thirst but taking inventory of the dryness of her life experience that she was existing in.

Look at what the woman had to face in the matter of moments: why she thirsted, how to quench her thirst, what had caused her to thirst, who could and would provide the resolution to her thirstiness. She had tried to fill her waterpot with emotional attachments with five husbands and a sixth man that wasn't hers. The reality was that she needed to extend herself to the living God who provided living water that could supply all her needs and ensure that she would never thirst again. Jesus saw that her motive necessitated His exposure of her life story.

Wow, I can just imagine this woman standing there without pretense or posturing consumed with the awesomeness of Jesus's presence, seeing her life unfold before her very eyes. Jesus had met her where she was and empowered her to take a hard look at her story without fear of reprisal or condemnation. She could finally be free of the burden of shame and blame. See, that is the presence that we all need to look for in our relationship with Christ—a relationship without barriers or pretense, a relationship that is accessible and honest.

The woman heard Jesus by the Spirit and power of His words, and she wasted no time in true repentance and worship. Her story came to light. And in her encounter with Jesus, her story came to life. The power of her experience enabled her to recognize to whom she had encountered—the Messiah! She recognized what she had been taught that the Messiah would come, and he would explain everything had come to fruition at her well experience. And from this encounter with this man at the well, she believed him because He, the Messiah, was able to provide the details of her reality as well as offer the healing that was so desperately needed in her situation.

Her enthusiasm was unmatched! Her healing and deliverance had come with great exuberance and joy. She wanted everyone to know. This man, the Messiah, had told her everything about herself, and He empowered her with the freedom she needed to live her life completely. And the Bible records that she just couldn't keep it to herself, that she ran and told everyone that would listen to come see this man that told her everything about herself—He truly was the Messiah. And this testimony caused many to believe.

The woman's well experience gave her life and liberty. She was now free from fear of her past and shame of her present. She could now testify just what the Lord had done for her. This is a message of hope for all us. We all experience life wells that are full of real-life situations and circumstances. We dip into wells that are watered with temptations and sins. We draw from wells that keep us drinking from pots that corrupt and defile us. Like our Samaritan woman, we can find hope, strength, and assurance that God sent forth His Son to meet us at our well experiences. We no longer have to keep dipping from wells that lead us to continue to thirst for things that will never satisfy or quench our thirst. We can draw from Jesus's saving grace and love. He is there to offer you the cup of salvation and the gift of eternal love and life.

The First Lady Proclaims: This Is My Story Too!

A First Lady of any congregation is not a role that many dream of as a young girl. When asked in elementary school what you want to be when you grow up, I wager to say, you want to find many little girls raising their hands, saying, "I want to be a First Lady of a church!" Needless to say, in many denominations, First Ladies are the go-to woman of the church, the point of contact for the pastor, the first responders to everything that goes wrong with the women, which also extends to being responsible for the wrong tie that the pastor wears to a worship experience.

First Ladies are misunderstood and misinterpreted. So many meet the role with ambiguity and resistance. Some just fake it to make it. Like Lady Barbara who has existed in the role for more than twenty-five years at a rural church where everybody knows everybody, she has been operating in her role, unintentional for quite some time. Lady Barbara would be described as being trapped between two realities: her church facade and her lived reality.

The day and life of Lady Barbara is always filled with errands, meetings, and to-do-list items. And this day was no different. First Lady Barbara arrived at the meeting ten minutes late, which was customary for her persona. She always made a not-so subtle entrance, whether it was meetings or the worship service. For Lady Barbara, unbeknownst to others, this was an intentional act of behavior. She enjoyed the focus being on her. Whether it was her new weave or the new outfit she was adorning, she made sure it was the outer exterior that others paid attention too and not what was going on behind the facade she emulated. Consciously or subconsciously, Lady Barbara modeled this motto: "Always show your best face." She believed that you give this type of appearance statement because you wanted to leave no one room gossiping or suspecting that anything could be deeper going on in your life when you are in the public. Lady Barbara wanted people to be enamored by what they saw without ever trying to dig deeper into what was tucked away.

Lady Barbara's backstory was interesting, and she enjoyed speaking about how she became the wife of a pastor. She married Pastor Graham after dating him briefly. She had lived a few counties over where he was pastoring at the time. Pastor Graham had frequently done preaching assignments in her local area. She ended up at one of his preaching engagements, and they met at the fellowship after one of the services. They hit it off. After a few more brief encounters, Pastor Graham and Barbara felt that the relationship could end up in marriage, and it did. By all appearances, the couple seemed to be a match made in heaven. They settled into their new relationship. They were the model Christian couple for many to marvel and model after.

Over the years, Lady Barbara settled into the day-to-day activities and routines of First Lady responsibilities. The responsibilities were trifold. She was the First Lady of the church, First Lady to her husband, and First Lady to her family. All three required her to always be on point without the consideration that she may be in a state of her own lack of self-awareness of needing to be "first" to herself.

First Lady had joined the First Lady committees and groups of the church and community. She made sure to attend conferences and workshops that related to effective service as a First Lady. She recalled at one conference she attended early on that one of the presenters told a group of First Ladies to "never let the congregation see you sweat." Barbara took this advice to heart, and she painstakingly presented herself in that way over the years. Lady Barbara did a great job in masking behind First Lady duties and responsibilities. She was skilled in overcompensating with service to our family and community. Only Barbara understood how much effort this took. But what would make Lady Barbara go to such great lengths to be center stage for everyone without really allowing people to see what was underneath? The reality was behind the backstory of her marriage to Pastor Graham. There was another story line that was untold.

First Lady Barbara had wrestled with this secret for years. She considered the fact that, every day, she risked that this part of her life would be exposed. She often considered how she would handle the nuances of her lived trauma becoming knowledgeable to the ones she loved and who were the closest to her. What if her real story got out, and the high esteem she had worked hard to secure came crashing down? Barbara had buried this secret in the far recesses of her mind intentionally; and over the years, she had become emotionally detached that it even happened to her. Now pushing forty-five years of age, she was becoming more anxious for some reason about what had happened to her when she was a child. She had begun to have more and more visions of the incident, which didn't really make sense. She wasn't sure what was triggering these images, but she knew she needed to do more work in suppressing thoughts and feelings that were attached to the incident.

When she was thirteen years old, Barbara was molested by her uncle. What started as what she believed as being her uncle's favorite niece ended up being a period in her life, bringing forth shame, guilt, and yes, a child. Barbara was impregnated by her uncle. Barbara disclosed what happened to her to her parents; but being in a small close-knit community, the family decided to handle the molestation and incest privately.

The uncle was confronted by Barbara's father. The family has not spoken to him since this day. However, none of this reconciled what happened to Barbara's innocence. Barbara was not afforded the opportunity to get justice for what had occurred. She received no counseling, which was definitely needed. The family swept the incident under the rug. Barbara concealed the pregnancy for nine months from her friends and other family members.

Her parents went to great lengths to make sure that her child was not further humiliated or shamed as they believed they were doing the right thing. Barbara remembered the day she went into labor; she was put into the car, and her mom drove her to a midwife's home a few towns over to deliver the baby. She really didn't have an opportunity to bond with her child because her mom had already arranged that the child would be given away.

Barbara's parents decided that they would give her child to a family member who could not have children of their own. They had made up an elaborate tale of how now fourteen-year-old Barbara was having a baby; and to spare her further embarrassment, the family was looking to have the child raised by someone else. Because Barbara always felt a sense of guilt that her molestation was her fault, she went along with the story line and buried the incident within. Barbara and the child were raised as cousins.

What a burden to carry. Lady Barbara attempted many times to tell her story through the years; however, she couldn't find the words to make the real-life experience come to light. Lady Barbara went to great lengths to hold onto her secret. Only a few people knew her secret: the perpetrator, her parents, and her husband. The cousins that were raising the child didn't even know how the child was conceived. They were just privy that Barbara found herself pregnant and that the family needed to cover the indiscretion up. The cousins agreed to raise the child as their own. It made for a resolution to a horrible and dark problem.

But how many times have we heard the adage "whatever is done in the dark will come to light." The perils of tragedy hit home; the cousin/son was in a terrible accident. He lost a lot of blood and needed a blood transfusion. As customary, the family members were all asked to be tested. The young man's parents frantically got in touch with Lady Barbara's parents to tell them what had transpired.

Lady Barbara was sitting, having coffee and reading the Word when the phone rang. It was her mother. She explained to Barbara what had happened to the young man and that he needed a blood transfusion. Lady Barbara, who they knew would be spot-on match for the procedure, went into panic mode. The moment she heard, she was in shock and in fear. What she had so masterfully concealed was now about to be uncovered and disclosed to many. Lady Barbara wasn't emotionally, psychologically, or spiritually ready for this. She informed her mom that she needed to talk to Graham first, but she also knew that her decision was time sensitive.

Lady Barbara was torn. She was trying hard to figure out how to accomplish the request without exposing the backstory of her life. She knew what she had presented for so long to her family, her community, more importantly in her role as First Lady of a leading church in her community. Lady Barbara had for years circled around her secret without allowing it to be exposed. She knew the best ways to change the narratives during any conversation that dealt with childhood trauma, infidelities, or unmasking fears. She had become stately in her position, and this would rock the very foundation of what she had presented for years, or at least she thought.

As Lady Barbara pondered her real-life situation, she thought about a similar encounter that a woman had with Jesus, a Samaritan woman who met Jesus at the well one day who was shrouded with her own secrets. This Samaritan woman's life issues were such that she would rather go fetch her water during the heat of the day unde-tected with a false sense of anonymity. Even though people thought they knew her story concerning her five husbands and the current one she was shacking with, this woman had lived her life within the confines of cultural, religious, and societal mores. This story could parallel to the life of a woman from a contemporary perspective who lived in the shadows of her own shame, fear, and guilt.

Lady Barbara could relate. Her secret caused her shame. Her secret overwhelmed her with fear and rejection. Her secret kept her isolated from allowing others in. Lady Barbara could just imagine how this woman would experience such a public encounter with Jesus and how apprehensive she felt as Jesus engaged her. The Samaritan's woman encounter was a vivid indication of how one would avoid coming to grips with their not-so-pleasant life experiences, past and present. No one knew why she had these various men in her life, although people speculated how she came to be the talk of the town. Could it have been she got passed down among the men in her husband's family? Could it have been that she needed a way to be safe in a society where women were treated like chattel? Could it be that she felt she needed that security of a man, and she was afraid to be alone? Whatever the circumstance or the situation, the Samaritan woman's story resonated in Lady Barbara's spirit because she alone knew why her secret was worth keeping a secret and believing its exposure would destroy her.

Although the circumstances were different in its details, Lady Barbara knew that her secret was drowned in the well of her pretense, denial, and fear. She needed God to certainly bring forth healing and deliverance so she could be empowered to tell her story without the garment of shame and guilt attached. She needed the Holy Spirit to empower her in giving voice to her story. She needed her well to be emptied of the sediments and impurities that clogged her for so long. She desired to experience the free-flowing gift of peace, joy, and unconditional love that only Jesus could give.

Lady Barbara recognized in the Samaritan woman's exchange with Jesus as a gift of forgiveness. She needed to forgive herself for not allowing the truth to come forth, although as a child, she couldn't understand the secret's impact on her life. Barbara needed to be liberated from the grip of shame and guilt. Her well needed to be drained, and her faith needed to be increased by the power of God's Spirit.

Although Lady Barbara did not follow through with the request, she sought help so she could come to terms with what had occurred to her. Lady Barbara began counseling. The counselor was able to help her gain voice about her victimization as well as recognizing the blessing of being a survivor. She knew that she had placed so much dirt of pain and shame over her situation in order to bury the acknowledgement of its existence. She recognized that it would take time to shovel the years of denial, hurt, and pain away.

One day, after months of therapy, Barbara asked her husband to call for a family meeting with their children. She wanted them together so that she could tell them the story of her childhood. She met with her parents and the cousins that were raising her son. She decided that it was time to heal. Although she has not had the courage to face her perpetrator, Lady Barbara had the strength that only God can provide to face the saga of secrecy that attempted to entrap her for years.

First Lady Barbara's life is fuller now. She is using her testimony to empower other women in her church, community, and with others who are survivors of rape, incest, and abuse. First Lady Barbara ministers to many this simple message: "Secrecy will entrap you at the well of hurt and pain, but Jesus offers a liberating experience through the power of the Holy Spirit."

CHAPTER 2

THE PREACHER PROCLAIMS: FROM BARRENNESS TO BLESSED!

And they rose up in the morning early, and
worshipped before the Lord, and returned, and
came to their house to Ramah: and Elkanah knew
Hannah his wife; and the Lord remembered her.

−1 Samuel 1:19 KJV

OFTENTIMES IN OUR lives, we find ourselves experiencing events that bring about horrific consequences and tragedies. Some events, trials, and encounters are going to make us feel that we are standing still in time. We feel as though we are without the ability to move forward. We may feel as though we are bogged down in a deep place of barrenness. I've experienced it myself where my ability to plant or to harvest is stagnated because of life's invasions. Emotionally, I am a wreck. Physically, I am depleted. Spiritually, I am still born.

As we mature in the things of life experiences, there will be times we will experience loss and longing, despair and desperation, brokenness and barrenness. But I've come to serve notice that even at these times, God is right there. Believe me, there are those who can't see how God is there as a loving Father when experiencing loss or despair. How can God be there to really soothe the pangs of brokenness and barrenness?

Sometimes we see people go through, yet does their witness truly contextualize the God that led David by still waters? We all have relatable experiences, yet in our text, we meet a woman who has an issue that is heavily laced in secrecy, disappointment, guilt, and shame.

Many of us may struggle to see ourselves in this particular text, yet there may be women and men out there who have experienced a level of barrenness that impacted them spiritually as well as physically. The story opens up with introductions. There was a certain man from Ramathaim, a Zuphite, named Elkanah, who was from the hill country of Ephraim. He had two wives; one was called Hannah and the other Peninnah. Peninnah had children, but Hannah had none. Yet Elkanah loved Hannah. This love was shown each time they made the pilgrimage to Shiloh to worship. To Peninnah, he would give portions of meat to her and the sons and daughters; but to Hannah, he gave a double portion because he loved her even though she was barren. She physically could not conceive children.

Elkanah loved his Hannah, yet the love was compromised, she believed, because of her lack of self-worth for being barren as well as the constant household battle between her and Peninnah. The love Elkanah possessed for Hannah was real, but there was strife within the household. Hannah's life had some topsy-turvy stuff going on.

Hannah understood the cultural and religious aspects of being a barren woman in her community. Barrenness, not a socially relevant topic, wasn't a conversation that was easily addressed or discussed. Barrenness medically represented of course the inability to bring forth a child; yet culturally and religiously, it meant something even more, the inability to manifest the very relevance that one was created for, what God created *woman* for.

Hannah had to live with barrenness, which in her culture, defined her; described her; designated her. A woman within this patriarchal culture saw that a woman's truest ability as well as calling was to procreate, to bear children, bring forth the legacy of a family. But Hannah could not! The Bible does not record why she was barren or how she became barren. Her reality was that she couldn't have children, yet the other woman to whom her husband was married too had several.

Many see the word "barren" as one-dimensional, representing a childless woman. However, I see that this term can also fit the description to much that we experience. We all experience degrees of barrenness in our lives, especially on our faith journey. There are those who longed for breakthroughs to come forth. However, no matter how hard they pressed, the same return produces itself—no breakthrough, no harvest. The yield is not fruitful.

Physical barrenness is reminisced to the fig tree absent of its fruit, which caused Jesus to curse the tree for not producing what it was designed to do. The story chronicled in Matthew 21:18–22, as well as Mark 11:12–14 depicts a powerful scene with Jesus. Some commentaries agree that the story with Jesus rebuking the fig tree took place on two separate occasions, which is not an impossibility. This story is symbolic for us! The moral should be what we practice in our lives. When we have things or people in our lives who don't produce their intended purpose in our lives, we should be ready to cut them off. Why did Jesus curse the fig tree if the scripture denotes that it was not the right season? The answer is found in the study of the characteristics of fig trees. The fruit of the fig tree generally appears before the leaves. And because the fruit is green, it blends in with the leaves right up until it is almost ripe. Therefore, when Jesus saw the leaves, He expected it to have fruit. The presence of a fruitful fig tree was a symbol of blessing and prosperity. Symbolically, the fig tree represented the spiritual deadness of Israel, who were religious outwardly with all the sacrifices and ceremonies yet spiritually barren because of sin. So barrenness can be a direct correlation to your sinful state, leaving you empty and depleted from the things of God and the gift of His Spirit.

Hannah's existence was shrouded in barrenness. The Bible does not indicate the details of her situation. We are only provided in verse 5 the gravity of her situation: "The Lord had shut up her womb" (1 Samuel 1:5 KJV). Barrenness was her lived reality. When she woke up, she was barren. When she went to bed, she was barren. When she made love to her husband, she was barren. When she walked to the market square with other women and their children, she reflected the obvious; she was the barren one. Barrenness was what she was characterized as; barrenness was her identification. Every mood depicted her state of barrenness; every emotion exemplified the barrenness she had.

Now Hannah didn't hold the corner office to a barren existence. Barrenness was a problem that many matriarchs encountered. Abraham loved his wife Sara, but she was barren before God opened her womb and blessed her with Isaac. Isaac loved his wife, Rebekah. She comforted him after the death of his mother, and he loved her with all his heart; but she was barren before the Lord opened her womb and blessed her with twins, Esau and Jacob. Jacob loved Rachel. He loved her so much that he worked for his uncle Laban for fourteen years, but Rachel's womb was closed. But God remembered Rachel and opened her womb, and she bore their son, Joseph.

And so, Hannah's story is relatable. She was married to a man who loved her, but the love she had for him was not complete because she felt the inadequacies of her barrenness. She lived under the scrutiny of society and the shame of cultural influences that determined her worth based on her ability to produce heirs for her family.

So here we were, Hannah childless without the possibility of having a child of her own. And to add insult to injury, there existed, within her same sanctuary, a space for the other wife of her husband, Peninnah. Elkanah's second wife was blessed to be able to bear children. She had what Hannah did not. Peninnah had an heir, a legitimate legacy for her husband through her womb.

The dysfunction of this situation! Can you imagine living every day in a household where you should feel like the queen, but you were reminded that you couldn't give what was necessary to carry forth the generation? Can you fathom what Hannah was feeling, wanting the respect of a mother, but realizing that you were no better than the concubine? On the surface, Peninnah was the source of all the friction. I mean, she was the one who constantly provoked and irritated Hannah day after day, moment after moment. The Bible records that Peninnah's provoking brought Hannah to tears.

Peninnah enjoyed the personal fulfillment and social status that came with bearing children. She was reaping the harvest of being the woman that could give Elkanah what he wished most. But I believe that life for Peninnah was not very fulfilling. Yes, she was able to bear children, but how embroiled was life for her living within a household with a man who really did not love her? I can just imagine that she spent a lot of lonely nights crying herself to sleep because she realized she was married to someone who did not share the same level of affection that she had for him. I am sure she questioned the worth of her marriage because he only knew her when he needed to procreate.

Unfortunately, there are some sisters who live under this same type of overshadowing situation, the Peninnah syndrome, saddled in relationships that are ulterior-motive driven, entangled in relationships that are one-sided in affections and emotions. Masquerading in relationships that presents themselves as authentic, yet in reality, it is just a fake existence. Peninnah and Hannah both lived with their own internal turmoil, varying in degrees of pain and emptiness.

Hannah needed to find a solution. She needed to find a remedy to her situation. Yes, Elkanah professed undying love. He gave her a double part of the sacrifice just in the hopes to lift her countenance. Yet Elkanah's attempts to resolve her real-life issue did not bring Hannah comfort. The Word declares that Hannah was in deep anguish, crying bitterly as she prayed to the Lord, making a vow that "if you will look upon my sorrow and answer my prayer and give me a son, then I will give him back to you. He will be yours for his entire lifetime, and as a sign that he has been dedicated to the Lord, his hair will never be cut" (1 Samuel 1:10–11). Her answer was a petition. Her solution was a prayer. Her resolution was a promise.

Hannah poured out her grief to God. She was so immersed in her plea that she had not noticed that the priest Eli was watching. She was so consumed by her grief and sorrow that Eli thought she was drunk. She was not drunk. She was just praying out of her pain. She was praying out of her heartbreak. She was praying out of her resentfulness. She was praying out her tumultuous circumstance. She was praying out of her hopelessness.

There is something about praying from a place of pain. As painful as the stigma of barrenness that Hannah was living through, she prayed. As painful as the constant badgering she experienced from

Peninnah, Hannah prayed. As painful as Elkanah's limited understanding of how she felt, Hannah prayed. Eli responded to her anguish, to her outcry of pain. The priest, after hearing her teary and anguished request, told her to go in peace. He promised that the Lord would honor her request as she had asked.

Hannah, woman of great sorrow, responded as a woman of great faith. She rose from her pain. She got up from her sorrow. She moved from bitterness with the assurance of promise and with the assurance that her life had purpose. She got up wiping the tears from her face. She returned home and, I suspect, with a new attitude. She was no longer sad. She was no longer downcast. She had a song in her heart. She had a new pep in her step. She knew in her heart that the Lord was going to turn her bitterness into blissfulness and her barrenness into blessedness.

The Lord remembered Hannah and opened her womb and gave her a son. She named him Samuel, saying, "Because I asked the Lord for him." God remembered her in her bitterness. God responded to her barrenness. Jehovah-Jireh heard her and supplied what she needed. El Shaddai, God Almighty, saw her and remembered her. In spite all that she had endured, she was blissfully blessed.

Barrenness did not have the last word. Bitterness did not create a gulf between her and God. She prayed, and God answered. She sought the Lord, and He remembered her. Elkanah knew Hannah, and she bore a son. She named him Samuel, for she said, "I asked the Lord for him." The Lord turned Hannah's barren situation to a blessed experience. And watch how God turns your barrenness to blessedness as well.

THE FIRST LADY PROCLAIMS: I WAS BARREN, BUT NOW I AM BLESSED!

Once a month, on the third Thursday evening, First Lady Michelle meets for prayer with a few sisters from her church. They gather to pray for the needs of each other, as well hearing the petitions that come forth on behalf of others that have requested prayer. On this particular Thursday, it was her time to lead the group. To focus their time, they typically opened with a discussion of a prominent woman from the Bible, discussed the relatable aspects of the woman's life, had prayer, and then adjourned. Assignments of the biblical women were given in advance and were assigned by the women's ministry's president. Lady Michelle was assigned the story of Hannah from 1 Samuel 1:1–19.

Most who have read the story of Hannah find encouragement and hope. Hannah's story chronicles the life journey of a woman who was barren and desperately wanted to give her husband a child. We are able share a glimpse of what many would describe as that forever love between a man and a woman. Hannah's story also narrates the flip side of her lived reality. She was a woman in sorrow and who felt that her inability to bear children dictated who she was as a woman, a story that gives perspective of a woman's life that is multidimensional in scope. The story of Hannah depicts a woman's life journeying through love, anguish, pain, resentment, and hope.

For Lady Michelle, Hannah's story was too relatable in context. It was a passage that had always presented its own level of discomfort and sadness. She identified with Hannah from that place of being unable to fulfill, which she believed the natural process for a woman's existence—to bear children. She was barren.

Lady Michelle and Pastor Mike had tried several times to have a child. They went to several fertility doctors who gave them the same diagnosis. She was unable to conceive, and the only alternative is adoption. Lady Michelle had never discussed the emotional or spiritual toil this had on her for years. She resisted discussing how the inability to conceive left her void and empty. She knew that Pastor

Mike loved her endlessly, but she also felt that she was denying him and their marriage the one thing that truly made them a family and the model what many believed was the perfect pastor's family. To add to Lady Michelle's anguish, there existed within her as well a level of resentment. Pastor Mike was married before, and he had children from his previous marriage. Although Lady Michelle loved her stepchildren, it remained an undisputable fact that she was unable to give Pastor Mike children.

As Lady Michelle entered the room, the ladies were engaging in light conversations, catching up on each other's busy lives. Lady Michelle always made it a habit to interact with each lady that was in attendance. She enjoyed being a hands-on First Lady. She wanted the women to feel a sense of ease during their sessions. Many of the ladies often discussed the most vulnerable aspects of their lives, so it was important to make the time to hear from each other, allowing this time to be a safe place for sharing.

After some time of sharing, the fellowship segment segued into highlighting their topic. The time began for Lady Michelle to present. She opened with prayer and read the focus scripture: 1 Samuel 1:1–19. She provided an exegesis of the text and its nuances as it related to cultural practices. Lady Michelle also spoke about the text's relatability to women who face similar situations. She pushed herself through the story as best she could, holding back any emotional schism she was experiencing at the time. She sat in her chair, resisting not to disclose what was resonating deep within her. So Lady Michelle struggled through the text. She couldn't bring to allow herself to be vulnerable to the text or to the women. Her inner voice kept speaking to her, rationalizing the need for secrecy and the inner shame she felt because of her barrenness. The meeting was adjourned after a brief discussion. They prayed, and Lady Michelle immediately left to grieve alone.

The ride home was quiet for her. She didn't listen to music. She didn't call her husband to chat on the ride. She just got lost in her feelings of self-worthlessness and sorrow. She knew she needed that time to get it together, to mask her hurt and pain. She needed the time to commune with herself and God.

Many couples deal with infertility. This subject is often deemed taboo in the Christian community. It is rarely discussed in the context of espousing the nuances biblically, spiritually, as well as culturally for families. Most couples feel a sense of embarrassment and/or shame concerning the subject matter. Typically, questions arise from family members, friends, coworkers inquiring when will the couple have children. Many women and/or couples provide plausible reasons to why they haven't had children, yet many may feel inadequate and guilty. Lady Michelle knew too well what that sense of inadequacy and guilt felt like.

Lady Michelle and her beloved Pastor Mike married years after both experienced terrible first marriages. They were serious about their faith as well as their relationship with God. After a brief period of dating, they knew that God had ordained their love and marriage. Pastor Mike had three children from his first marriage. His relationship with his children was beautiful. Lady Michelle appreciated the love that he had with his children. She also appreciated how they accepted her into their lives.

Pastor Mike's relationship with his former wife was of mutual respect and harmony. Watching both of them parenting the children was a model for many blended families. The children would visit every other weekend and spend half of the summer with them. Lady Michelle did her best in connecting with the children on every level. However, Lady Michelle struggled with bonding with them to a place that she felt a real maternal connection.

Lady Michelle had no qualms about Pastor Mike's faithfulness to their marriage. However, years of not being able to conceive, she felt a lack of confidence and doubt that their love could sustain a childless marriage. Lady Michelle's emotional unrest caused her levels of stress, tension, and insecurity.

She festered over what people considered as the model church family. She so desired to have the full package: God, husband, children, and life. She believed that a pastor and First Lady of a church were to represent unity, family, and faith; yet her key ingredient of children was not there. Although she was a stepmother, it still did not give her the true definition or model of what family should exemplify.

Lady Michelle felt that her position as First Lady was stymied because she did not exemplify the biblical principle of "being fruitful and multiplying." How could she talk about being a mother without experiencing motherhood? How could she comment affectionately about the joys of motherhood when she lacked that level of intimacy with her stepchildren? Although she had perpetrated the majority of the time as the altogether First Lady, she knew, at some point, she would have to face her internal demons about being a childless woman and wife.

Lady Michelle grew weary internally each time she had to engage the subject of children or having children of her own. With such spiritual and emotional distress with the subject area and lived reality, Lady Michelle continued to have unresolved issues concerning her barrenness and the lack of maternal connection with her stepchildren.

Lady Michelle was good at compartmentalizing her life. So it is without question she knew how to tuck all this away until the next time she would have to confront family, children, or infertility. Lady Michelle and Pastor Mike continued their life journey of working the nuances of family, church, and community. As life would happen and to their dismay, the family received some devasting news. Her husband's first wife had stage 4 cancer, and the doctors gave her only a few weeks to live. This was not news that the family was expecting or ready to process. There were immediate decisions that had to be made as it related to the children and their care. Of course, without question, the children would now come to be with her and Pastor Mike.

Lady Michelle was feeling overwhelmed by her emotions. She was going through internal misgivings. Her new reality of life has now added another level of complexity to her internal struggle. As they began the legality of assuming custody of the children, Lady Michelle's was emotionally triggered, having now to make decisions about becoming a full-time mom. She was now having to address her misgivings and addressing her thoughts about her own inability to conceive.

She was now faced with how to go forward with her stepchildren who would soon become a greater responsibility for her and her husband. She was in a vulnerable place. She knew she needed to purge herself of what had laid within her for so long. How could she be vulnerable to her husband at this time when emotions were heightened over dealing with his former's wife illness and the children coming to live with them full-time? How could she burden him with, she had rationalized for so long, her own insecurity? How could she give voice to what had been painful for her for quite some time without sounding petty or resentful?

Lady Michelle decided that the time had come to discuss this thorn in her side with her husband. It was not an easy conversation; and actually, it took her husband by surprise. He was not aware that she was experiencing anxiety and anxiousness over the years as it related to parenting and not being able to have children of her own.

After days of talking, turning into silence, praying, and giving way to open reflection, Pastor Mike suggested that they go to couple therapy to deal with the issues concerning her inability to conceive as well as to discuss his children coming to live with them. He felt it was necessary for Lady Michelle to give voice in becoming a full-time mother to her stepchildren. Admittingly so, at first, Lady Michelle found the sessions difficult and emotionally draining. However, she knew that in order to gain victory and healing, she had to stick this out and be assured that God was with her and that her husband supported her.

Like all of life's situations and circumstances, there comes a time that one has to acknowledge the big elephant in the room. The sessions were at times contentious. The post conversations at home were at times extremely difficult to have. Things didn't magically get better overnight, but Lady Michelle and Pastor Mike were willing to do the work of healing.

Lady Michelle worked hard to arrive at a place of both healing and wholeness. The therapy, along with her deep faith in God, enabled and empowered her to find validation in what she was feeling. The sessions gave her time to talk about how the new position as a full-time mother was now becoming a reality. She discussed with the counselor what necessary steps would benefit her in how to transition into this role as she made the necessary adjustments that would benefit the family as a whole. Lady Michelle was able to develop positive coping skills to deal with her sense of inadequacy, shame, and guilt.

Lady Michelle so appreciated the in-the-moment way that her husband supported her journey. Pastor Mike wanted what would be best for the love of his life. He knew that in order for them to be healed, they both had to work together in building and strengthening their bonds. Lady Michelle and Pastor Mike were confident that the journey would meet roadblocks at time, but the destination would be certain: "a life full of love and commitment."

CHAPTER 3

THE PREACHER PROCLAIMS: VASHTI'S VIRTUE!

But when the attendants delivered the king's command, Queen Vashti refused to come. Then the king became furious and burned with anger. Since it was customary for the king to consult experts in matters of law and justice, he spoke with the wise men who understood the times and were closest to the king—Karshena, Shethar, Admatha, Tarshish, Meres, Marsena and Memukan, the seven nobles of Persia and Media who had special access to the king and were highest in the kingdom. "According to law, what must be done to Queen Vashti?" he asked. "She has not obeyed the command of King Xerxes that the eunuchs have taken to her." Then Memukan replied in the presence of the king and the nobles, "Queen Vashti has done wrong, not only against the king but also against all the nobles and the peoples of all the provinces of King Xerxes. For the queen's conduct will become known to all the women, and so they will despise their husbands and say, 'King Xerxes commanded Queen Vashti to be brought before him, but she would not come.' This very day the Persian and Median women of the nobility who have heard about the queen's conduct will respond to all the king's nobles in the same way. There will be no end of disrespect and discord. "Therefore, if it pleases the king, let him issue a royal decree and let it be written in the laws of Persia and

Media, which cannot be repealed, that Vashti is never again to enter the presence of King Xerxes. Also let the king give her royal position to someone else who is better than she. Then when the king's edict is proclaimed throughout all his vast realm, all the women will respect their husbands, from the least to the greatest." The king and his nobles were pleased with this advice, so the king did as Memukan proposed. He sent dispatches to all parts of the kingdom, to each province in its own script and to each people in their own language, proclaiming that every man should be ruler over his own household, using his native tongue.

–Esther 1:12–22 NIV

I N AMERICA, 2017 was dubbed as *year of the woman*. The MeToo movement became a hashtag on every social media platform, which led to widespread conversation and activism among women from every hue, social-economic class, racial demographic, and well as geographic location. This movement hit the reset button for women's rights and issues. MeToo allowed a wide berth to be opened, addressing concerns and experiences of women ranging from sexual assault to workplace harassment. This movement propelled the issues of women who felt hostage to the social, political, and institutional conservatism that held them at bay with rules and laws that seemingly were meant only to "keep women in place." Nothing like this had seen so much notoriety since the time of the woman suffrage movement.

The MeToo movement, the women's suffrage movement, as well as other women-empowerment movements can find their origin from many of our biblical stories. From Sarai to Ruth, from Huldah to the widow of Zarephath, from Mary to Priscilla, biblical women have shaped the progression of this movement. Interestingly enough, Queen Vashti, from the book of Esther, made her own imprint as well. Sermons have documented the rise of Queen Esther and minimized the relevance of Queen Vasthi's moment. Queen Vashti's story is short; yet it is a reminder that *no* means *no* and that we, as women of faith, can stand up and speak truth to power.

The story begins in Susa, a citadel of the Persian Empire under King Ahasuerus. In the third year of his reign, King Ahasuerus, for 180 days, made a show of his wealth to all who were present. Everyone who was in the region was invited to the palace. At the end of this time, he provided a seven-day banquet for all the people who were in the citadel, from the greatest to the least.

The banquet was lavish, with only the choice foods extended to his invited guest, as well as strong drink which was plentiful. Interestingly enough, the drinking was according to the law, for the king had given orders to each official according to his household that he should do according to each person's desires (Esther 1:8). There was no order to drink, but each person could drink as much as they so desired. And while the king was attending the merriment of his guest, Queen Vashti also gave a banquet for the women.

This king, in his arrogance, was determined to show off the riches of his royal glory and the splendor of his great majesty. Arrogance led him to invite all of the princes of the land. People traveled far, and King Ahasuerus wasted no expense in showing off his extreme wealth and excess. King Ahasuerus made this show of his glory and majesty. In modern chronology, this expansive and expensive soiree equates to six months of festivities and folly. The scripture also tells us that when the event was tapering off, he wanted to show more his extravagance. He gave a banquet that lasted for seven days. So for all those who were still at the citadel, the party was far from being over. There was much food, lots of drinking, and merriment.

We all recognize the haphazard choices that are made when we make choices under the influence. We will dare not say that assault or infringements upon a woman or anyone's personhood is legitimated by alcohol or substance abuse. We have to see how over the top excess can bolster a sense of entitlement and infringement as it relates to the King's behavior.

The scriptures tell us that the king's heart was merry with wine when he made his command for Queen Vashti to come. His mind was influenced by days of drinking and excess of food, what the millennials would call "turnt up!" His judgment was that of privilege and entitlement. I would dare say that the king's mother did not provide wise council that was told to King Lemuel in Proverbs 31:3–5, "Do not give your strength to women, or your ways to that which destroys kings. It is not for kings, O Lemuel, it is not for kings to drink wine, or for rulers to desire strong drink, for they will drink and forget what is decreed, and pervert the rights of all the afflicted." Needless to say, the king was being guided by his own desires and fleshly lust. He wanted the envy of those who were there, and he called forth for his wife, Queen Vashti.

But who was Queen Vasthi? Within the book of Esther, Queen Vashti seemingly played a rather minor character in the biblical narrative. However, her story has made her both hero and villain in the world of philosophical genderism. Biblically, Vashti was the queen to Ahasuerus who ruled over the lands from India to Ethiopia. There is no mention of Vashti, nor of Queen Esther, in any historical works outside of scripture. Although this does not negate the possibility of either the historicity of these women or the events, most scholars suggest the account is an etiology (a story that answers a question—a pedagogical device).

On day seven, apparently, after too much revelry and drinking, the king boasted of the beauty of his queen and sent messengers to fetch her so he could display her before the partygoers. In the biblical account, we read of the royal command: "To bring Queen Vashti before the king, wearing the royal crown, in order to show the peoples and the officials her beauty" (Esther 1:11). She was to appear adorned with nothing but her crown. This, for the king, was a way to boast of his ability to pick only the finest of women.

The request was not met with expediency. Vashti refused and resisted coming into the king's presence. The king felt slighted. He was infuriated, and matters only worsen because others were in the king's ear. The Bible states that the princes that were there offered an opinion to what had just transpired between the king and the queen. Their meddling gave rise to suggesting that "this deed of the queen will be made known to all women, causing them to look with contempt on their husbands, since they will say, 'King Ahasuerus commanded Queen Vashti to be brought before him, and she did not come.' This very day the noble ladies of Persia and Media who have heard of the queen's behavior will rebel against the king's officials, and there will be no end of contempt and wrath!" (Esther 1:17–18). In other words, the princes and other men surmised that their wives would feel empowered to disobey them because of Queen Vashti's disobedience.

Was Queen Vashti a hero or villain? Queen Vashti, to many, may seem to be drawn into the characterization as villain. In the Jewish faith, much has been made of Vashti's "disobedience." In many of the commentaries, Vashti is painted as the disobedient wife. She was the reason for the marital strife that existed in their relationship. The patriarchal culture (male dominated) would much prefer demure, obedient, and subservient women. But Vashti was not one of those. At this point in time, she demonstrated none of these characteristics. Instead, Vashti was depicted as a disobedient wife. Never mind that to obey her husband would have been to shed her of every ounce of dignity. She chose to validate herself with one simple word, *no*! A hard no.

On the other hand, there are those who see Vashti as a hero, a champion of women, and women's rights everywhere. To many proponents, Vashti represents the epitome of self-respect and self-determination. This woman stood her ground. The fact that Vashti refused to obey such a heinous request by no means discredits her. Queen Vashti's refusal demonstrates the insensitivity and immorality of her husband. Queen Vashti's "no" meant that she saw value within herself. For the King, however, her "no" represented disrespect and dishonor.

It is important to know that when motives are not righteous or conducted in humility than it should be anticipated that consequences and resistance may occur. So often out of arrogance and entitlement, people are moved to command and demand from those who they deem are beneath them. Case in point, King Ahasuerus made a request to call for Queen Vashti to present herself to him and his guest. His motive was not to summon her to come to serve as hostess for the event or to bid greetings to his guest; his motive was to pimp her beauty. He wanted to use her as a pawn from his treasured possessions. He called her to show off what he had.

From the patriarchal context of this story, it was rightly known that women were seen as possessions and property. He did have patriarchal as well as royal rights to summon her and to will her to do what he wanted her to do, but Queen Vashti took notable objection to his request. She resisted.

During this time, women were seen as inferior to men. Women in the Hebrew Scriptures (Old Testament) were viewed with limited power and access. Restrictions in ancient Israel included the following: Unmarried women were not allowed to leave the home of their father without permission. Married women were not allowed to leave the home of their husband without permission. They were normally restricted to roles of little or no authority. They could not testify in court. They could not appear in public venues. They were not allowed to talk to strangers. They had to be doubly veiled when they left their homes. Women were no more of value than to the property of animals in the field. So in his arrogance, the king wanted the queen to appear for his pleasure and the pleasure of the other men assembled.

But Queen Vashti refused. Her resistance, her refusal, sent shock waves in the kingdom. As we see this story differently, we see how Queen Vashti's story pushed the reset button for us, as women, and our ability to stand our ground. We all need to begin to view the story differently from a different perspective.

Many, including myself, have always taught and preached that Queen V was disobedient and showed no reverence to her king or position. But as I have evolved as a woman, especially as a woman of color, my womanistic views have evolved to see that this was not disobedience; rather it was more of resistance to an unethical and immoral request. This was more than just no reverence for her position but rather her understanding of the virtue of her position.

I'm sure, for six months, the king had bragged about the beauty of the queen and his ability to will her and everyone else to succumb to his authority. I'm sure he was boastful of how his fleet of women far exceeded any woman in the providence. And to add to the fact that no one had the courage to argue against his assertions, his boastfulness was accepted and respected by the attendees.

Queen Vashti sent her response back to the king. Verse 12 states, "But when they conveyed the king's order to Queen Vashti, she refused to come. This made the king furious, and he burned with anger." He was mad. I will submit that he was more angry from embarrassment than by her refusal. Who does she think she is, refusing the king's request? And then, to add insult to injury, his boys didn't help by igging him on with the assertion that the queen's refusal would bring about a movement within the kingdom from the women who would see this as a power play. But from my assertion, she was only being virtuous; she was helping him when he didn't see that he needed help!

King Ahasuerus's pride caused him to make a blanket decision and decree. His prideful behavior, influenced by partying, his boys, his understanding of a woman's worth, and status in his culture led him to make a hasty and rash decision. The text states that, in response to Queen V's refusal, the king became "very angry and his wrath burned within him" (Esther 1:12). His anger got the better of him. He turned to his wise men and asked what could be done by the law to Vashti.

Certainly, what she had done must be against the law! The wise men gave the king what he wanted to hear at that moment, a way to deal with Vashti, taking to a place that addressed his ego, pride, and vanity. They fed him the notion that her behavior against the king would influence the women to disrespect their husbands within the providence. So they made a political decision that they assumed would be for the betterment of all the people. Esther 1:21 says, "This word pleased the king and the princes, and the king did as Memucan proposed." All of the men sitting there together were pleased by this idea—a room full of bruised egos, seeking to posture themselves as the testosterone-in-chiefs, making themselves and the king feel better.

So the decree went forth, and Queen Vashti was forever banished. We need to remember that King Ahasuerus was not a godly man. God was using his nation to bring Judah to repentance so the remnant could return. God used this ungodly man and possibly

Vashti's seemingly disrespectful behavior as an approach to show us all something about virtue, respect, and humility.

Queen Vashti may have been the prop for the king on many occasions, but this time was different. The Bible doesn't tell us why she refused, but she came to herself. She would not surrender to political or personal pressure. She would not be a victim to patriarchal definitions or cultural interpretations. She would stand as a woman of virtue and as a woman who knew her worth. She would stand as a woman who knew the power of her voice and willing to receive the consequences for right and righteousness.

We can learn from the realities of this story and its impact on our lives as we attempt to navigate who we are as women of God in this world. Society still limits the number of us who crack the glass ceiling. Male dominance continues to resist our voice and leadership in places that have been ordained for our arrival. Government continues to want to control what we do to our bodies, what we think, and how we respond. Queen V, the queen of all queens, showed us a virtuous way on how to rise to the occasion of power, authority, and righteousness.

THE FIRST LADY PROCLAIMS: TONIA'S VIRTUE CAN'T BE QUESTIONED!

Historically, first ladies of most churches have been at home—wives and mothers. Not to diminish their status, the role of at-home wives and mothers was just as demanding. Over the last thirty years or so, this has swiftly transitioned. Bivocational First Ladies are just as notable as bivocational pastors. With the rising cost of everything—insurance, food, childcare, housing, education, and the list goes on and on—a one-person, breadwinner mantra is nostalgic at best. First Ladies are now just as high profiled as their pastor-husband counterparts.

First Lady Tonia was no different than any other independent woman of the twenty-first century. She was a successful entrepreneur and a pillar of the community. She was strong, tenacious, savvy, creative, and independent. All these attributes were attributed to her. And those same attributes were ascribed to her in her role as First Lady. Lady Tonia didn't split hairs with you. She was as direct as it came. Now for some, this was a definite positive and applauded attribute. However, for others, this seemed arrogant and a bit off-putting.

As fierce as Lady Tonia was outside the church community, she never compromised that same zeal or energy in the household of faith. Many of those in the congregation would describe Lady Tonia as a woman who walked in a spirit of excellence, which knowingly excelled the congregation and its appeal in the local community, as well as with other churches. It was not unusual that when one spoke of Milestone Christian Fellowship Church (MCC), you would hear Bishop Rodney and Lady Tonia in the same breath. Their names were synonymous to each other.

To the outside, Bishop and Lady Tonia depicted the ideal power couple of the city. They just celebrated twenty years of marriage with an elegant affair. The three children were finally at a place of interdependence. They were all in high school, so this really freed up time for Lady Tonia. Finally, they were reaching a period in their lives where they could live out a sense of freedom in their ministry and community activism. To onlookers, their lives looked at ease. They seemed to be preparing for and anticipating the life of empty nesters.

They both had impressive backgrounds, mastering in educational achievements and excelling in career endeavors. Lady Tonia always made it a point to spotlight Bishop, no matter the occasion. Not an event nor conversation or personal dialogue she was part of, she would give accolades to Bishop. You had no doubt knowing that she loved her husband. It was evident that she loved him, and she was enamored with this man of God.

However, during this year of their relationship, Lady Tonia sensed a decline in their relationship. The relationship was becoming more divisive. Bishop was not as affectionate. The affection was not reciprocated by him toward her. It was almost as if he detested being around her. The same level of respect was being lost in their daily interactions. Bishop had grown critical at home of her, and this was beginning to spill out at meetings at church, as well as during public events.

Bishop was becoming increasingly hostile anytime Lady Tonia's attributes, notoriety, and contributions were spotlighted in the church and community. At first, she would just chuckle it off as him being his comedic self; yet the critical critique was becoming increasingly inappropriate. It was now impacting her position as First Lady and as matriarch of the family.

Lady Tonia was feeling a sense of awkwardness at church and at home. She was now experiencing the residuals of her husband's demeaning tone and attitude. It was now spilling onto others, treating her curtly and with disrespect. She was trying to pray herself through this situation. Although she confronted Bishop numerous times, it seemed to only ramp up his insults and lack of empathy and compassion. She was at a loss to what to do. She tried to reassure him often of her love as well as commitment to their ministry work.

The growing intolerance of her by Bishop was causing Lady Tonia to lose confidence in herself. She wanted to understand what had changed in her marriage to make her husband treat her in such a distant and disrespectful way. Lady Tonia suggested counseling on numerous occasions to no avail. This left her beyond belief.

After months of painful arguments, tearful exchanges, Lady Tonia decided to confide what she was experiencing with a close sister friend. Sister Alice suggested that she seek counseling on her own. She decided this would give her an opportunity to deal with how this had impacted her as well as address the growing anger and hurt that was brewing within. Lady Tonia's sessions were eye-opening.

She was able to find the validation of self-worth that was being tainted by the constant put-downs and demeaning behaviors from Bishop. She also was able to process the emotional abuse that she was living through daily. The counselor empowered Lady Tonia in seeing that the constant belittling from her husband was more about his insecurity and inadequacy than hers. Lady Tonia realized that she had to find a way to resolve this conflict or she would have to find a way to walk away from a growing disconnect within her relationship.

Bishop decided that he would finally go to counseling with her. The sessions were at first heated with passionate posturing as well as tearful admissions. Bishop acknowledged the pain that his wife had been experiencing over the months, yet he could not reconcile that he was the cause of her injury. He felt as though the tension within the marriage was due to the lack of Lady Tonia's inability to operate in her place as just First Lady. He saw her growing visibility in the community was really the problem and that she was now trying to emulate that same appeal in his congregation. He wanted her to understand that she was just First Lady and not his copastor. Bishop acknowledged that, over years, he had accepted that people assumed they were copartnering in ministry; however, now he was at a place that he needed Lady Tonia to be his wife. He wanted the church to see him and his contribution alone in the ministry.

The counseling sessions were eye-opening for both of them. She began to really assess her role in her marriage, church, and community from a different perspective the way Bishop perceived expectations. She began to ponder and assess whether or not she was willing or could make the necessary steps to become subordinate to the ideals of her husband, aligning herself to the parameters of being the bishop's First Lady.

She was at a crossroad. Nothing in their lives had ever made her feel that life was hopeless. She knew she had to make a decision in order for her life to move forward. Lady Tonia could not accept that God would ordain her to surrender her goals, gifts, and talents that He had blessed her with. She could not fathom being that woman having no voice, no visible purpose or position in her church or community. She couldn't accept the idea that she was going to have to align herself to the marching orders of a man who wanted her to sit pretty, look pretty, and keep a smile on your face—portrayal that bolstered his perceived idea of how a First Lady should be.

Months went by, and the family struggled to regain familial composure. Lady Tonia came to the realization that her twenty-plus-year relationship was over and that it was time for her and Bishop to dissolve their marriage. The intensity of a love, ministry, and marriage had now fizzled to a flicker that could not be reignited. No matter what the real issue was, that allowed Lady Tonia and Bishop to arrive at this place could not be scripted in a thirty-second sound bit. Unresolved feelings, tension, and unspoken anger caused the unraveling of a marriage and ministry.

Lady Tonia desired that this would be an amicable dissolution; however, Bishop became even the more hostile. Lady Tonia moved to an adjoining town and reluctantly allowed the boys to remain with their father to complete their high school experience. She is active in the lives of her sons and remains committed to them. Her ministry and business continue to strive. She witnesses to other women, reminding them that "one's light shines for the glory of God and God alone!"

CHAPTER 4

THE PREACHER PROCLAIMS: THE DOMINO EFFECT OF DESPERATION

Now when Jesus had crossed over by the boat to the
other side, a great multitude gathered to Him; and he
was by the sea. And behold, one of the rulers of the
synagogue came, Jarius by name. And when he saw
Him, he fell at His feet and begged Him earnestly,
saying, "My little daughter lies at the point of death.
Come and lay your hands on her, that she may be
healed, and she will live." So, Jesus went with him, and
a great multitude followed Him and thronged Him.

—Mark 5:21–24 NKJV

MANY OF US have heard the term or terminology "domino effect," but what does that really mean? The domino
effect is defined as a chain reaction when one event sets
off a chain of similar or unrelated events. It typically refers to a linked
sequence of events where the time between successive events is rel-
atively short. So what that means is that when something happens,
and literally in short order, it produces something else to occur.

We see this domino effect exemplified daily. We've seen this in
the Word often when it relates to women. The domino effect occurs
when Queen Vashti stands up for her MeToo rights, but she gets
dethrone while another woman assumes the position and brings
the authority of God's power to the throne. Domino effect occurs

when accusations concerning moral character by the religious leaders occurs because of a sinful act. But Jesus drew words in the sand, possibly writing about their mess. Jesus forgave the woman's sins while the naysayers scattered like roaches. When the domino effect occurs, there can't be but a change, whether that change is positive, negative, or both simultaneously.

In our text, we are introduced right away to a daddy arriving at the side of the lake to meet Jesus. Now, Jesus had just gotten there, and the crowd had already formed. But this religious leader, named Jairus, in urgency and desperation, approached Jesus. He met Jesus, not negating his position or his status. He didn't come in the cloak of secrecy. The Bible says he was a synagogue leader. And when he said Jesus, he fell at his feet with a request.

Jairus pleaded earnestly about his daughter. His daughter was home, dying. He was desperate for Jesus to make an emergency home visit. Let me tell you something, my sisters and brothers. When you are desperate, it doesn't matter what your occupation; it doesn't matter what your social status might be; it doesn't matter how much education you have; it doesn't matter how much income you have; political affiliation doesn't even have standing; when you are desperate, and when you need Jesus, when you know that your life is on the brink of destruction, you will seek out Jesus because you need Him to do what He does!

The fact of the matter is that desperation can only be defined as a person's ability to see that they are helpless and that it will take a greater source, a powerful resource, and undeniable force to get them out of their situation or circumstance. And the only source I know, the only resource I know that we can depend on, the only real deal force that can break down barriers and pull down strongholds, is Jesus, the Son of God who has all power.

The Bible says that Jesus went with him. And as they journeyed, a large crowd began to form and follow them. Yet in the midst of their journey, something unexpected occurred. A woman appeared in the crowd. Our narrator points out to us that this woman had been stricken with a blood issue for more than twelve years.

Now I just want to pause right here so I can remind you of what I told you about the domino effect. A domino effect occurs when one thing is happening, and it causes a chain of events to take place. So here we have Jairus in route to his home. Now I don't know if they were walking down Main Street, crossed over Warburton Avenue, took a right on Ashburton Avenue, and then a right on Nepperhan Avenue; but what I do know is that Jairus took a certain route, which led them down the street where a woman was there, contemplating how to encounter Jesus. The woman saw the massive crowd, and she joined the crowd because she didn't want to miss the opportunity to engage Jesus.

Pause here for a minute. I know your Mama always warned you about following the crowd. Your grandma told you, don't get involved in the crowd. Sometimes you need to assess the crowd. Always evaluate how the crowd is operating; what its purpose is; who they are supporting. This crowd was following Jesus who was in route to Jarius's house to save his dying daughter's life. And just like that, the dying daughter and a father's desperation began a domino effect for a miracle.

In our story, within the crowd, a woman was gravely impacted with a blood issue. For twelve years, she dealt with the issue which, in her case, was a societal and financial curse. She had a blood issue which, needless to say, had also both cultural and religious ramifications. The stigma for having such a medical malady dictated certain religious rituals, laws, as well as cultural rules on how she could interact with the community and even her family. So in reality, social distancing and sheltering in place ain't nothing new. This woman was tied to this, and she lived it for twelve years.

However, today, something prompted her to take the risk and venture outside. Something moved her to see what was happening outside. The Bible says she heard Jesus was in town. I would offer that her desperation motivated her to find out what Jesus could do about her situation.

The story unfolds, and we find that the woman got close enough to Jesus, so close that she was able to touch his clothes. Powerful! The woman touched Jesus, and immediately her blood issue stopped. Just like that, what had kept her ostracized was gone. Just like that, what kept her subjugated was gone. What kept her bound disappeared. What kept her believing wholeness was not a possibility or plausibility was gone. And this began one part of the domino effect from one man's desperation to a woman being healed.

Yet even as great as this appears, the domino effect can present a positive as well as cause a negative response. The Bible says that in the midst of this victory for this woman, when there should have been a praise outbreak, the crowd in pandemonium, a shift occurred. Jesus asked who touched Him. He asked so He could address the miracle that He knew had just occurred.

Yet the disciples caught an attitude. The disciples presented Jesus with a "whatcha asking that from us" for response. They persisted in speaking to Jesus in a way that showed their lack of full knowledge of who they were really traveling with. However, Jesus was not disturbed, nor did He even entertain their negative posture. As He spoke to the crowd, the woman came to him and fell at his feet. Jesus spoke to her, "Daughter, your faith has healed you. Go in peace and be freed from your suffering."

In this one-dimensional experience, this one-dimensional exchange, something else was occurring. Jairus got notification that his daughter had died. What a devasting blow to this daddy. His daughter was now gone. Jesus was not moved by the news. He urged Jairus to continue on with their journey. Jesus went to the house with only three of the disciples, not a big crowd, just enough to witness the miracle.

I can't but be amazed how this is going to play out when a domino effect of desperation intersects with the power of Jesus Christ. Here we had this desperate daddy, a desperate woman with a blood issue, a desperate baby girl. When a domino effect of desperation comes in threes, I am crazy enough to know what three symbolizes in the spirit realm. Three represents divine wholeness. Three represents completeness. Three represents perfection. This is a lesson for us all to remember that when we are desperate, when we give it over to Jesus, a divine stamp of completion and fulfillment is on our situation.

Jesus took Mommy and Daddy in the child's room and took her by the hand and said to her, "Little girl, get up!" The Bible says that the girl got up and started walking around. So I'm saying to you, get up! Get up and watch God perform a miracle. Get up activate the plans that he has given you. Get up and live out the promises of God over your life! Get on up and begin walking in your calling. Get up and begin walking out your purpose.

A domino effect of desperation leads to a trifecta miracle and blessing. Not only was Daddy blessed with his daughter being healed, a daughter was blessed to live, and another daughter/woman with a blood issue was made whole. I don't know what the popular feeling is about situations that are desperate, but there are some out there that will take a little desperation in their lives as long as God is there in the midst. They will take chances with Jesus any day with their circumstances and situations as long as they know that Jesus is in the midst with His trifecta miracles and blessings of deliverance, wholeness, and transformation.

THE FIRST LADY PROCLAIMS: IT COMES IN THREES!

Another day, another checklist of routines complete, and now I can retire and think on those things that I meant to get too. Lady Shana has always been called a multitasker, a get-it-done type of woman. She doesn't know how she keeps up with herself, not to mention with the hectic schedule of ministerial duties with her husband, Elder Robert. Everyone in her circle knows that when you are a First Lady and an ordained minister, the demands on your time and ministry can be sometimes overwhelming. And Lady Shana was right there.

This year had become particularly overburdensome because there were personal issues that became more critical to address. First

Lady was feeling a loss of interest in traditional ministry work. She was becoming more isolated as it related to her feelings about how and where she believed God was calling her to. She knew that if she told Elder Robert what she was feeling, he would God-talk her feelings away. They have been serving in ministry together for more than twenty-five years.

Lady Shana had the heart of a servant. She was committed to ministry in the urban center of the city. She and her husband decided years ago, early on in their ministry, to forego the traditional church placement locations. They usually rented spaces in their local city so that they could be in the mix of the critical realities of urban habitation. They had been leasing a space for more than ten years, and this had become a place that saw much growth and sustainability for ministry work.

Among many of her hats, Lady Shana was also actively involved in the chaplain ministry at their local children's hospital. She volunteered three days a week as a chaplain assistant. She really enjoyed her work there. The more she engaged in chaplaincy work, the more her spirit was settled in this line of ministry service. This was becoming a tug within her to explore chaplain ministry more fully.

Recently, while working, the head of hospital's chaplain services came to her and asked if she would be interested in a full-time position as director of chaplain services. This position would come available by September. He was retiring, and she was the first person that came to his mind to apply for the position. Lady Shana was mixed with emotions. Excited, yes, however she immediately thought about how this would impact her family, the church, and more importantly, her husband. This was a decision not to be taken lightly.

Since timing meant a lot in Lady Shana's life, she had decided to put off her conversation until later with her husband about the new career/ministry opportunity. Lady Shana was holding off her conversation with her husband while praying for direction and clarity from God. She remained even the more detailed in her work at the church, though putting plans in place so that the area of ministries to which she was assigned would be able to operate with less oversight without losing accountability and effectiveness in case of her departure. Her well-thought-out plan seemed to be working. However, just like that, something would happen that would seemingly cripple her hope of a new ministry opportunity.

Like life does, it evolves, and sometimes it spirals out of control. Lady Shana's life was now seemingly being turned upside down, inside out. Expectation of blessings had now intersected with several unexpected burdens and problems. At a time where she felt like she was about to shift into a new level of ministry, life, and profession, her husband was diagnosed with colon cancer. And to add more injury to this life-altering event, they received devasting news that the church was facing economic calamity because the property owner of the building was facing foreclosure proceedings.

Lady Shana's lived reality was in fact life altering. Lady Shana could not but reflect momentarily of how she and her husband had acquired the property in the first place. However, the reflection could not linger; everything was coming unglued at the seams. Lady Shana's ministerial future, her husband's illness, and the life of the church were now hanging in the balance.

What was she to do? What decision could be made that would bring about positive outcomes for everyone and everything involved? Early May became a time of intense obligation, and Lady Shana's emotional state was, needless to say, overwhelming. She found ways to juggle all that was now before her and upon her. She decided that the first thing that must happen was that she had to figure out how to deal with the crisis with her husband. Lady Shana knew that her first attention had to be about her husband and his medical issues. Lady Shana and Elder had two children. Both of the children lived in different states with families of their own. Neither of them had the heart to ask one or both to come help them out, so they relied on each other. Members of the church, friends, and some distant relatives were eager to assist when and where they could.

After several appointments with the oncologist, Lady Shana and her husband found out that the cancer was in an early stage. His prognosis looked great. Because the doctor was able to detect it in time, his treatment plan would not have to be so invasive. The doctors were assured that Elder Robert would be able to beat the cancer with a regimented treatment of chemo, radiation, and oral medication. This gave the family a sense of relief and hope.

Lady Shana was taking charge, however the responsibility of everything was breathing down her neck. She felt better in handling her husband's crisis with the support of those who had offered. The church's crisis continued to loom over them, and the hospital had reached out to schedule an interview. Lady Shana had almost lost hope of that blessing becoming a reality. She had left that discussion with Elder Robert on the back burner because, with everything they were now facing, a new job didn't seem that important or a priority. Lady Shana had left a voice message for the director to decline the offer.

Although Lady Shana felt life had thrown her two bad curveballs, she also realized that her life with Robert was that of complete honesty and trust. He often would walk by her and pause to ask what was troubling her. Lady Shana would not give a direct response, but her husband knew that something more was amidst. Lady Shana was hoping she had left the chaplain work behind.

As careful as she could be, Lady Shana avoided the topic of the offer because, as far as she was concerned, it needed not to be discussed since she had declined the offer. One day, while she was going over some papers pertaining to the church, her phone rang, and she asked Elder Robert to get it. When Elder Robert answered the phone, it was the children's hospital. The director stated that he was calling because he received a message that Lady Shana would not be accepting consideration for the chaplain's position, and he was calling to see if he could persuade her in changing her mind. To Elder Robert's shock and surprise, he told the director that he would have his wife call him back.

Lady Shana was entangled with the responsibilities that were before her, so she hadn't noticed that Elder Robert entered the study. She was so laser focused on the paperwork for the building. She was not prepared for the conversation that was to take place. Elder Robert informed her concerning the conversation he just had with the director of chaplaincy at the hospital. He wanted her to reconsider and set up an interview within a few days. Elder Robert was bewildered in why Lady Shana had not discussed it with him and why she would turn down the position.

Lady Shana explained that this was a hard issue to discuss since they were faced with some many obstacles right now. Elder Robert was empathetic with her reasoning; however, he didn't appreciate the fact that she felt that it was too much of a transition for the family and the ministry without giving him the opportunity to have an opinion in the matter.

Elder Robert began ministering to Lady Shana. He explained that blessings come and also life issues. He stated that we have to be reminded that when the Lord sends the rain, there may also be flooding; yet we should never overlook the rainbows that appear. Lady Shana felt an overwhelming sense of relief. She began telling Elder Robert how she felt emotionally conflicted because of the issues of his health and the prospect of losing the church. She felt as though there was no need to look for a rainbow in the midst of their flood. Elder Robert was right there with a right-now word for his wife: "We can do all things through Him who gives us strength" (Philippians 4:13). He reminded her that God is working things out for them, even if she didn't feel or see it right now. He stated that at this critical time, they both needed to have faith and be thankful. And finally, Elder Robert reminded her of their motto for marriage and ministry: "Where faith and hope grow, miracles blossom."

Lady Shana took to heart all that her husband was sharing. She could see how God had already begun the miracle with her husband's cancer diagnosis being at its early stage. The doctors had assured them that the prognosis was favorable and that they could treat Elder Robert. This was a true relief for the couple.

They could also see how God's favor was also being instrumental in the issue of the building. Lady Shana and Elder Robert were working with the bank that was preparing foreclosure procedures on the property. The couple had spoken to the owner to see if the ministry could actually purchase the building with a small business loan. The owner and the bank felt this was a great possibility. The couple began the process immediately.

Both Lady Shana and Elder Robert could actually see the actuality of hope in the midst of their storm. Lady Shana decided that she would call the director back and schedule the interview for the position. Elder Robert was quite happy that Lady Shana would make the call.

Lady Shana was interviewed the following week. She prepared earnestly for the interview. For Lady Shana, landing this position would offer resolution to her internal conflict about her own ministerial direction. She was both anxious and relieved that the storms the family was engulfed in were no match for God's sovereignty. She knew, with Robert as her cheerleader and support, this would be a battle that could only be victorious.

CHAPTER 5

A First Lady's Personal Story: Shattering My Silence!— Dr. Elaine Sanders

LIFE CAN BECOME complicated quickly. Dr. Elaine stands years later, whole and secure in her path as an ordained minister. However, the journey did not begin that way, walking in the office of First Lady. Based on Dr. Elaine's critique of her life experiences, she wouldn't say that her story was by any means different from other women who serve as First Lady of a church; however, the ending does bring forth a different perspective over against what it may appear like to others from the outside looking in. Let me introduce to you First Lady Elaine from her own voice that began when she decided her silence had to be shattered.

Elaine had grown up in the church. So she knew church. It was at the age sixteen that Elaine began to take seriously her relationship with God. As she matured, her spiritual journey and experiences were manifesting so much in her life. She had finally moved from religion to a solid relationship with God.

This became even more evident when the Lord blessed her to marry a pastor, a man of God. She was excited about her new journey. Here she was, twenty-six years old, and God had sure enough positioned her in a right relationship. She wanted more than anything to serve the Lord, her husband, her pastor, and her community. She believed that life would be great because she was marrying her soul mate. They were "biblically" equally yoked. They both loved God, and the passion was evident in their commitment to ministry.

Admittingly so, Elaine shared how she revered this man of God. He was well versed in the word of God. The power of God was upon his life. She would often say to herself, "Lord, you gave me your best." As the years progressed, Elaine experienced a shift in her relationship with God. Elaine describes it this way, "I went from having the Word explained and taught, to understanding the Word for myself and then being elevated to proclaim the Word of God to others."

Elaine was excited. She saw her and her husband as this dynamic couple in the body of Christ. Elaine and her husband were becoming more and more notable in their call in ministry. She was seeing the Lord move in their lives.

Ministry was exploding. She was thrilled, and she thought he was too. It was not until they were invited to minister internationally that she recognized their relationship began to shift. This was her first time leaving the country, and how exciting it was that it was God's assignment.

Elaine had been preparing for this for over six months. She wanted the Word to be just right. She knew the awesome power and anointing that rested on the host bishop as well as her husband, so she wanted to bring pride to both of them for doing a good, theological, sound job. She wanted to make God and her husband proud.

When they arrived, the power of God was moving, and you could feel the divine presence of God there. Here she was, First Lady and a minister, about to embark upon an experience most women preachers could only dream of. They had finally arrived. Elaine was so excited about ministering. On the night she ministered, the power of God fell in that place, and people were being healed and delivered. She was in awe of God's power. And what made this occasion even more joyous for Elaine was having her husband by her side. One would think this would have been a great time as they celebrated the power of God together. To be able to minister with such power and authority was more than Elaine could have anticipated.

After the service was over, Elaine and her husband headed back to the hotel. When they arrived back to their hotel, her husband-pastor stopped speaking to her. She couldn't believe it. She had come to another country with the greatest hope of new ministry and new growth in the things of God, excited and anticipating this wonderful experience to be one for the books, and he was not speaking to her! Elaine mustered up enough courage and mental strength to ask him what was wrong. The reply was not what she was expecting. Her husband-pastor stated that "he did not like that God used her more than he used him." Wow! Jealousy and competition had come to her front door.

To be honest, Elaine admitted that she did not know how to process this information. She was hurt. She quickly realized though that as long as she was the cheerleader in the relationship, cheering him on, boasting of his accomplishments, he was fine. She recalled saying to God, "I rather keep my marriage then my ministry." This was her unselfish proclamation.

Unfortunately, this was not a one-time event where Elaine felt that her husband-pastor was in competition with her. Elaine expressed her lack of competitiveness drive within herself. This behavior was so foreign especially because she wholeheartedly believed that marriage brought a sense of oneness, and they were supposed to be on the same team.

She believed God would help him see this. She trusted that everything would work out just fine. A passage of scripture that she hang her belief and trust on was in Philippians 2:2: "Make my joy complete by being of the same mind, having the same love (toward one another), knit together in spirit, intent on one purpose [and living a life that reflects your faith and spreads the gospel—the good news—regarding salvation though faith in Christ]" (Amplified Bible). It was her hope that he would see the value of their collectiveness, especially in ministry.

Nevertheless, Elaine remained believing that things would get better. However, the marriage was hitting more lows than highs, more valleys than mountaintops. She believed or thought that building their family would strengthen their relationship.

In strengthening the relationship, they began growing their family. The couple was blessed with three children. Each child was born out of need and love. Their second child was born with multiple disabilities. One would think this would definitely bring about an inseparable bond. However, Elaine was left even more alone and shattered in the experience. She was left to handle all of the medical care and therapies of their precious blessing without his involvement. Needless to say, Elaine expressed often to the child with the disabilities that she was "her child."

Having three children was a handful. Having a child with disabilities intensified the parenting aspect. The life journey for their child was tiresome, wearisome, and anguishing. There were sleepless nights in the pediatric ICU with a minimum of eight days. She felt the burden and the need to go it alone. She was forced to care for the oldest, her middle with disabilities, a baby, and work full-time. She was overwhelmed, but she had to keep up the facade of togetherness. Her pastor husband wanted to portray a happy, well, put-together family to the outside world while inside we were broken and shattered.

This was an unimaginable situation for Elaine. The person who she thought would be a blessing for her life had turned out to be a total nightmare. Like any other married couple, they tried to salvage what was left from arguing, silence, and lack of trust. The couple tried several counselors; however, whenever they did not agree with him, they stopped going. Elaine discovered that there were so many insecurities within this man who she thought was all put together. No matter what she did right, he always found something wrong. There was never an encouraging word but readily a criticism, not a critique. Elaine felt the foundational shaking and shattering of her marriage. She was married to someone who not only lacked the support needed to raise a family but someone who could never celebrate her wins, the person who was supposed to be her life partner.

To Elaine's dismay, nothing was happening. It was as if God wasn't hearing her at all. She began seeking counsel with other First Ladies. Some would say, "Just pray, and God will make everything all right." And others actually could identify with her present struggle. Elaine felt this was the first time people saw her and not the title. This was agonizing and causing Elaine to assess the benefits over against the repercussions of just walking away from everything. After much prayer and thought, Elaine decided to end the marriage. She was criticized and lost so-called friends in ministry. But guess what, she was okay because she had to reclaim her life back.

The decisive action came with mental health and emotional challenges. Elaine recalled the time she had to take pills for anxiety due to the marriage. In prayer, one day, God brought a scripture to her remembrance: "He came that I may have life and have it more abundantly." Elaine felt like she was dying within and knew that if she had to take a pill to stay in a marriage, there was something wrong.

The divorce process was very ugly; and to this day, the communication is not the best. The pastor's parting words to Elaine was that she broke up the family, and nobody would ever want her because she would be strapped with three children. Even in the dust of divorce, this man remained psychologically abusive. He really tried to plant every negative seed he could within her. Elaine jokingly admits though that the weapon was formed, but it did not prosper because God had her and her children the entire time.

Elaine is now eight years on the other side of her divorce. She has no regrets at all. Elaine said, "I learned, if you cannot be where you are celebrated, do not stay just to be tolerated. Reconciliation is always the first step, but you have to know when you have to count your losses and move on and be thankful for the things you gained from the relationship."

Elaine has three children who she absolutely adores. She is better, not bitter, because of her process. The victory came when she refused not to remain as a victim of her own circumstance and refused to remain silent. A part of her ministry gift is praying for pastors' wives. She is more than qualified to know the blessings and curses that come from sitting in that seat. But for Elaine, these days are filled with nothing but smiles. She has embraced the woman she is and rediscovered herself. Her message is simple: Enjoy your journey!

ABOUT THE AUTHOR

Reverend Margaret Fountain Coleman presently resides in Westchester County, New York. She is presently an elementary school educator, an ordained minister, podcast host, and published author. She has earned degrees from various colleges and universities over the course of her life in criminal justice, education, and ministry. Reverend Coleman is a sought-after preacher and teacher specifically on issues that face women spiritually and emotionally. Her ministry message encompasses a wholistic approach through the word of God. Reverend Coleman is the CEO and founder of Brand Yourself Ministries, LLC. She travels extensively, hosting women empowerment conferences. She hosts a weekly podcast *Rev. Margaret's Monday Moments*, which can be found on various streaming platforms. She also ministers daily on Facebook and Instagram "Rev. Margaret Moments," a daily inspirational moment that brings dialogue, encouragement, and consultation to women via social media. She can be found on Twitter (Margaret Coleman@ fountaincoleman) and TikTok (margaretcoleman773). Reverend Coleman is a published author.

Reverend Coleman is committed to her call to Christian ministry and the preaching of the gospel. She is dedicated to the ministry of those who are disenfranchised and marginalized. Her commitment to God and God's people is led and directed by the Holy Spirit. She is known as a woman of faith and a sojourner for justice.